# WONDERS
## OF THE WORLD

# The Great Barrier Reef

Other books in the Wonders of the World series include:

Easter Island Statues
Gems
Geysers
The Grand Canyon
Icebergs
Mummies
Niagara Falls
Pyramids
Quicksand
Sand Dunes
Sunken Treasures
King Tut's Tomb

# WONDERS OF THE WORLD

# The Great Barrier Reef

## Peggy J. Parks

**KIDHAVEN PRESS**
*An imprint of Thomson Gale, a part of The Thomson Corporation*

**THOMSON**
✳
™
**GALE**

Detroit • New York • San Francisco • San Diego • New Haven, Conn.
Waterville, Maine • London • Munich

*For more information, contact*
KidHaven Press
27500 Drake Rd.
Farmington Hills, MI 48331-3535
Or you can visit our Internet site at http://www.gale.com

| LIBRARY OF CONGRESS CATALOGING-IN-PUBLICATION DATA |
| --- |
| Parks, Peggy J.<br>    The great barrier reef / by Peggy J. Parks.<br>        p. cm. — (Wonders of the world)<br>Contents: Miles and miles of coral—It is alive—Disappearing reef—Danger lurks in the reef.<br>    Includes bibliographical references and index.<br>    ISBN 0-7377-2054-9 (alk. paper)<br>    I. Title. II. Wonders of the world (San Diego, Calif.) |

Printed in the United States of America

# CONTENTS

# Miles and Miles of Coral

Coral reefs are some of the most fascinating natural structures on earth. Often called underwater cities, these reefs are found throughout the world in shallow, tropical waters, as well as in the deep ocean. By far the largest and most remarkable of them all is Australia's Great Barrier Reef.

One of the Seven Wonders of the Natural World, the Great Barrier Reef is a miracle of nature. Its name suggests one continuous reef, but it is actually a reef system—a collection of more than three thousand individual reefs. Some are within twenty miles of the shore, while others are nearly a hundred miles out. The reefs are separated from land by a large body of seawater known as the Great Barrier Reef Lagoon. Beyond the reef system is the Coral Sea.

From its northernmost point, the Great Barrier Reef stretches along the eastern coastline of Queensland, Australia, for about thirteen hundred miles. That means it is nearly long enough to reach from top to bottom of the entire United States.

## The Story of Coral

One reason the Great Barrier Reef is so amazing is that it was built by tiny living creatures called **coral polyps**. These cousins of the jellyfish have a flowerlike appearance, so they were originally thought to be plants. Coral polyps may be as small as the head of a pin or as big as a dinner plate. They have tube-shaped bodies and

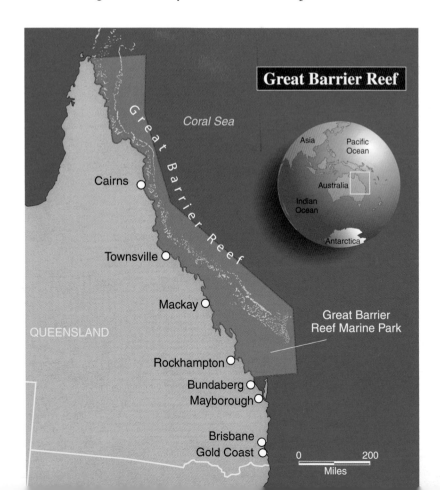

mouths that are surrounded by tentacles. Polyps are delicate creatures—but their tentacles are far from delicate. They are covered with stinging cells that polyps use like poisonous darts to catch and paralyze microscopic animals called **zooplankton**. Then their tentacles pass the food into their mouths.

The polyps that build coral reefs are called **stony corals**. They often live in colonies with thousands of other polyps. Stony corals build protective skeletons by extracting **calcium carbonate**—the same material found in teeth, bones, and shells—from the salty ocean

The coral reefs of the Great Barrier Reef are made from the skeletons of millions of tiny creatures called polyps.

waters in which they live. The polyps stay inside the skeletons when they are not feeding. When they die, their bodies decay but their skeletons remain behind. New polyps grow on top of their ancestors' carcasses and build their own skeletons. Over a long period of time, all the skeletons of a colony are woven together to form a reef. Certain types of algae grow between fragments of skeleton, which helps cement the reef together.

There are also many types of **soft coral** in the Great Barrier Reef. These creatures have tentacles like stony corals. However, most soft corals are not reef builders because they do not grow skeletons on the outside of their bodies. Instead, the polyps have tiny crystal-like structures called **sclerites** inside their bodies, which act as internal skeletons.

No one knows exactly how long it takes coral to grow. Some scientists believe it grows about one centimeter per year, which is just under half an inch. The National Oceanic and Atmospheric Administration (NOAA) believes it grows more slowly—about thirteen feet every thousand years, or a mere hundredth of an inch per year. That means it took hundreds of thousands of years for the enormous Great Barrier Reef to form.

## A Riot of Color

Coral reefs are spectacular places filled with vibrant colors. At first glance it appears that the color of stony coral comes from the skeletons, but they are actually white. The colors are created by the layer of coral polyps on the surface. The polyps have clear bodies, but

The algae that live inside the coral polyps produce a pigment that creates the vivid colors of the coral reefs.

living inside them are millions of microscopic algae cells known as **zooxanthellae** (pronounced zoh-zan-*thel*-ee). These algae produce a pigment that creates brilliant hues such as red, yellow, blue, and purple, and the colors show through the polyps' bodies.

The relationship between polyps and zooxanthellae is unusual because the creatures benefit equally from it. In a process known as **photosynthesis**, the algae use the sun's energy to convert **carbon dioxide** from the seawater into food and oxygen. The zooxanthellae share some of the nutrients with their polyp "hosts." The extra nutrition supercharges the polyps, helping them to produce skeletons at a much faster rate. In return, the polyps provide the zooxanthellae with a safe place to live.

Many soft corals are also brilliantly colored, but in most cases, their hues are caused by sclerites rather than zooxanthellae. Underwater photographer David Doubilet describes them: "Soft corals have a soft, feathery skeleton. Their thick branches . . . look like massive heads of broccoli in psychedelic colors: yellow, purple, pink, orange, and mauve."[1]

## From Bubbles to Fans

Some of the most interesting types of coral are named after the things they resemble. For example, bubble coral looks like a cluster of bubbles, staghorn coral looks like the pointy antlers of a deer, and daisy coral resembles a bouquet of flowers. Brain coral could be mistaken for a human brain—but it would be an enormous brain because the coral can grow to six and a half feet in diameter. Many other varieties such as pillar coral, mushroom coral, and organ pipe coral also bear a striking resemblance to their namesakes.

Another unusual species in the Great Barrier Reef is fire coral, which has long, pointed branches. Fire coral can deliver a burning sting to creatures (including scuba diving humans) that swim too close to it. Hydroid coral, which resembles a fern with feathery white leaves, is also known for its sharp sting. Sea rod coral looks like the spiky limbs of a pine tree, and purple sea fans spread out and wave gracefully beneath the water. Whip coral can be as thin as spaghetti or as thick as a human thumb. Some whip coral spiral away from a reef like giant corkscrews.

## Islands, Cays, and Ribbons

Throughout the immense stretch of the Great Barrier Reef, there are thousands of islands. Some, called continental islands, are the tops of mountains that have been covered by the sea. There are also reef islands, called **coral cays**, that were formed from the compacted debris of coral and shells. Over time, many of these islands were covered with vegetation, and some have developed lush tropical rain forests.

One unique tree that grows on some of the islands is the mangrove. Mangroves are called forests of the sea because they grow where the land and water meet. Unlike most other plants, they thrive in salty seawater. When the water is high and their roots are hidden, mangroves look similar to other tropical trees. But when the tide is out, they are unusual looking. The trees perch atop a thick mass of tangled, gnarly roots that stick far out of the ground.

Beachgoers enjoy an afternoon in the sun on one of the thousands of coral cays, or reef islands, found along the Great Barrier Reef.

All the coral reefs that make up the Great Barrier Reef have their own shape, size, and physical characteristics. **Ribbon reefs** run along the shoreline and are usually the closest to land. **Barrier reefs** also run parallel to the shore, but they are farther out. Their name comes from the barrier they form between the lagoon and the sea. **Patch reefs** are small coral formations that are scattered throughout shallow areas. **Platform reefs** grow in deep water and are circular or crescent shaped. **Fringing reefs** sometimes grow outward from the shoreline, but are most often found on the fringes of islands. **Atolls**, ring-shaped reefs that surround lagoons, often grow on the tops of underwater volcanoes.

## Nature's Gift

Nowhere on earth is there anything like the Great Barrier Reef. It is a place of beauty and mystery. Author Judith Wright shares her thoughts about this extraordinary natural

A scuba diver marvels at the many colors of a section of reef. The Great Barrier Reef is a place of great beauty and mystery.

phenomenon: "There are a few places in the world which [fulfill] the meaning of the word 'enchantment.' They not only delight the senses, but they cast a spell which can even affect the behaviour of human beings. . . . The Great Barrier Reef is one place which has that power."[2]

# It Is Alive!

**T**he coral species that live in the Great Barrier Reef are far from alone. The entire place is teeming with life, and there are enough colors to rival the most breathtaking rainbow. This vast underwater universe is constantly in motion, bustling with activity every second of the day and night.

## From Mini to Massive

More than two thousand varieties of fish live in the Great Barrier Reef's clear blue waters. One of the tiniest is the goby, a fish so small it is practically invisible when hiding in the branches of soft coral. Gobies are unusual because their body structures and internal organs are miniature replicas of the shark—even though sharks can be a million times their size.

More than two thousand kinds of fish live in the waters of the Great Barrier Reef, from the tiny goby to the large potato cod (pictured).

Some of the largest fish in the reef are the potato cods. They have pale bodies with dark speckles, much like a potato. Potato cods can grow up to six and a half feet long and weigh more than two hundred pounds. They are sneaky creatures that wait patiently behind clusters of coral until small fish or crabs swim by. Then they lunge out from their hiding place and grab their prey, swallowing it in one gulp.

The outer areas of the Great Barrier Reef are home to whale sharks, the world's largest fish. Whale sharks can be more than fifty feet long—longer than a city bus. Yet despite their intimidating size, they are gentle giants that have no teeth. That is not true, however, of some other sharks in the reef. For instance, the tiger shark is one of the Great Barrier Reef's most ferocious predators. These creatures are much smaller than whale sharks, but they have large razor-sharp teeth and are known for eating anything. The stomachs of captured tiger sharks have contained tires, car license plates, cans, plastic bottles, burlap sacks—and the remains of people.

## Neon, Polka Dots, and Stripes

Many fish in the Great Barrier Reef look as though they have been handpainted with an artist's brush. The coral cod has a reddish orange body that is peppered with vivid blue spots, and the long-snouted butterfly fish is neon yellow and black. Another colorful fish is the fairy basslet, which has fluttery deep blue fins, a purplish pink front, and a bright yellow back.

Some fish change the way they look in order to hide from enemies. The flat-shaped peacock sole is a master of camouflage. It can transform its appearance to match its surroundings by changing colors. If the surface on which it settles is polka-dotted or striped, the fish can actually create a matching pattern on its own body.

The clownfish, another expert at hiding, has a bright orange body trimmed with wide white stripes, so it looks like it is wearing a clown suit. Clownfish are partners with **sea anemones**, often called flowers of the sea. Sea anemones are creatures with stinging tentacles that are poisonous to most fish—but the clownfish is immune to their sting. At the first sign of danger, it rushes to the anemone and nestles safely inside its tentacles.

## From Giant Clams to Spanish Dancers

The Great Barrier Reef is also home to thousands of varieties of **mollusks**. They have soft bodies that are usually protected by shells. Some of the most familiar mollusks are snails, oysters, and scallops. One that lives in the reef is the giant clam, which can grow to four feet long and weigh up to five hundred pounds. These creatures are sometimes called killer clams or man-eating clams, but the nicknames have no basis in fact. In the past, some people thought the clam's huge shell could clamp down like a steel trap on a diver's leg or arm. Now it is known that giant clams close their shells so slowly that they do not pose much threat to humans.

The **nudibranch** is a mollusk that does not have a shell. Nudibranches are vividly colored sea snails whose shapes may be smooth, spiky, curly, or lumpy. One

Because it is immune to the sea anemone's poisonous sting, the clownfish can hide from danger in the anemone's tentacles.

type looks like a flower with huge feathery petals. Each nudibranch has its own distinctive color and pattern. Some are red, yellow, or creamy white, while others have brown speckles, blue stripes, or purple dots. The Spanish dancer is a nudibranch that appears to be wearing a red and white swirling skirt. When it is disturbed, it vigorously waves its body as if it were performing a dance.

Although the giant clam of the Great Barrier Reef may look threatening, it actually poses no danger to humans.

## Swimming Cows?

Another creature found in the Great Barrier Reef is the **dugong**. Sometimes called sea cows, dugongs are quiet, gentle animals. When they are swimming, they look similar to dolphins because of their fishlike shape, forked tail, and flippers. However, unlike dolphins and most other water mammals, dugongs are not carnivores. They eat only underwater plants such as algae and sea grasses that grow in warm, shallow waters. An adult dugong can eat more than eighty pounds of sea grass in one day.

Dugongs can grow to nearly ten feet long and weigh more than eight hundred pounds. They do not have many teeth, but they have two tusks in the front of their mouths, similar to those of elephants. As the tusks grow, they develop growth rings much like the rings of a tree. By examining the tusks, scientists have determined that dugongs live about seventy years.

## Creatures Abound

Many types of reptiles, such as sea snakes, lizards, and saltwater crocodiles, live in the Great Barrier Reef. There are also six species of sea turtles, including loggerheads, hawksbills, giant leatherbacks, and green sea turtles. Raine Island, in the northern part of the reef system, is one of the world's few breeding grounds for green sea turtles. David Doubilet once saw an enormous mass of these turtles as he flew above the island in an airplane. At first he thought he was seeing a cloud of algae, but then he realized what the "cloud" actually was:

as many as eighty thousand turtles that spread out over the shallow reefs and open water.

One intriguing reef dweller is the sea horse. These fish range from a tiny one inch to twelve inches long. They have curved bodies, tightly coiled tails, and heads that resemble a horse. Sea horses are especially unusual because of the way they produce their babies. The female sea horse deposits eggs into a pouch on the male, and that is where they are fertilized. After about two weeks in the father's pouch, the eggs hatch and develop into baby sea horses. So, the male sea horse actually "gives birth" to the babies.

## Venomous Creatures

Some Great Barrier Reef creatures are deadly. One of them, the box jellyfish, is the most venomous creature in the sea. Box jellyfish are a transparent blue color and have a box-shaped head. Dangling from their bodies are sixty tentacles that look like long strands of thin spaghetti. The tentacles are filled with poisonous stinging cells and if one even brushes against a human, it can be fatal.

The blue-ringed octopus is equally dangerous. The creature resembles a golf ball with a sharp beak and a tangle of long tentacles. When it is resting, its color is yellowish tan. However, if it feels threatened, its color becomes vivid yellow and blue rings on its body "light up" as though they were electrified. That is a warning that the octopus is about to strike—and there is enough venom inside its body to kill more than twenty adult humans within minutes.

The blue-ringed octopus is very poisonous. Its venom can kill more than twenty humans in just a few minutes.

The Great Barrier Reef is alive with creatures of every size, shape, and color. They may stay in one place, creep along the seafloor, or swim as fast as lightning. No two are exactly the same, but they all share one thing in common: They live together in the world's most vibrant and splendid underwater home.

# Disappearing Reef?

**T**he coral in the Great Barrier Reef took hundreds of thousands of years to form. Because it has withstood the test of time and grown so enormous over the years, it would be easy to assume that it can survive forever. It is seriously threatened, however—by nature as well as by humans.

## Nature Eating Nature Alive

One of the greatest threats to the Great Barrier Reef is from one of its part-time residents: the crown-of-thorns starfish. These creatures can grow to be nearly three feet in diameter. The tops of their bodies are covered with long, pointy, razor-sharp spines, which gives them a sinister appearance. Yet the biggest problem is not that the starfish look scary. It is their ability to destroy massive amounts of coral.

One crown-of-thorns starfish can devour huge sections of coral because of the strange way that it feeds. The creature's mouth is on the underside of its body. When it wants to eat, it pushes its huge stomach right out of its mouth. Then it spreads the stomach over a patch of coral that is as big as its whole body, and leaves the stomach there for about six hours. As the starfish feeds, it secretes enzymes that liquefy and digest the polyps. When it has finished eating, it simply pulls in its stomach and moves on to feed at the next patch of coral.

One of the biggest threats to the Great Barrier Reef is the crown-of-thorns starfish. This creature can devour huge sections of coral in a few hours.

All that is left behind is a bare white skeleton called a feeding scar.

Scientists think the crown-of-thorns starfish has existed on the Great Barrier Reef for thousands of years. However, the first major outbreak was not recorded until 1962. A huge number of the creatures suddenly appeared at Green Island, in the central area of the reef system, and they multiplied rapidly. Within two years about 80 percent of the island's coral was completely destroyed. Then the starfish disappeared as mysteriously as they had arrived. People were shocked—no one knew why the creatures had suddenly taken up residence

A satellite image shows a section of the Great Barrier Reef. The entire reef is threatened by global warming, as warmer water causes coral to lose their color and die.

there, whether they would come back, or if they could be stopped. In the following years there were serious outbreaks in other areas of the Great Barrier Reef.

For the past twenty years, scientists have studied the crown-of-thorns starfish and they now have a better understanding of it. But they are still unsure what causes outbreaks to occur, or exactly where the creatures will strike next. With continued research, they hope to find the answer to these and other questions. Until they do, the entire reef system is at risk.

## Coral Bleaching

The Great Barrier Reef is also threatened by ocean waters that continue to grow warmer. This is the result of **global warming**, a steady increase in the earth's temperature over a period of time. Even though scientists do not always agree on what causes global warming, it is a fact that the warming causes the oceans to heat up. Tropical waters such as those of the Great Barrier Reef are shallow, so they warm much more rapidly than deeper water.

When water temperatures become too high, corals lose their colors. That is because the warmer water causes the polyps to expel zooxanthellae. Once the algae cells have been expelled, the white skeletons show through the clear bodies of the polyps and the coral takes on a bleached appearance. If temperatures remain too high, the corals are vulnerable to disease, permanent damage, and death.

Before the 1980s coral bleaching in the Great Barrier Reef was not widespread. When it did occur, it was confined to small areas. During the past twenty years, however, bleaching has increased dramatically. For instance, the summer of 1998 was the hottest season ever recorded in Australia during the twentieth century. During that summer, history's worst outbreak of coral bleaching occurred throughout the Great Barrier Reef. Many reefs suffered damage that ranged from mild to severe. Then four years later an even more serious bleaching epidemic occurred. After the summer was over scientists studied more than six hundred reefs. Nearly 60 percent showed signs of mild to serious bleaching. Researchers hope that most of the reefs will be able to recover from the damage. There are some reefs, though, where that will not happen because up to 90 percent of the corals died.

## Water Pollution

Just as corals are vulnerable to warmer ocean waters, they are also affected by the quality of the water. In order to survive, corals must live in water that is clear and shallow. When large amounts of soil wash in from the land, sediments float down and settle on the coral. This blocks out the sunlight, which reduces photosynthesis and growth. The sediments can also smother the coral polyps so they die.

Increased sediment loads have become a problem in the Great Barrier Reef because of land development along the Queensland coast. In the past two hundred years, more than 50 percent of the territory has been completely cleared of vegetation. This was primarily to

This coral has been severely bleached as a result of changes in the salt content of the waters around the Great Barrier Reef.

create farmland for growing crops such as sugarcane and cotton, as well as for grazing livestock. Without trees and other vegetation to cover the land, it has become barren and vulnerable to erosion. So during heavy rains or severe floods, sediments are washed into the lagoon.

Another effect of coastal flooding is that freshwater from rivers and streams is swept into the lagoon's salt water. The result is a change in the water's natural **salinity**, or salt content. Coral reefs can only grow in salt water, and when their environment becomes less salty, bleaching can occur. The change in water salinity has led to severe coral bleaching in several areas of the Great Barrier Reef. One example is a fringing reef around an area known as Snapper Island. In 1998 half of the coral was killed as a result of freshwater flood runoff.

One way that agriculture contributes to water pollution in the Great Barrier Reef is the use of chemical fer-

**Coral Damage from Land Development**

1. Clearing land for agriculture and development makes the Great Barrier Reef vulnerable to water pollution.

2. Heavy rains and floods wash more soil sediment and chemical fertilizers into the lagoon along with freshwater from rivers and streams. The freshwater changes the salt content of the coral's environment.

3. Sediment smothers the coral polyps. Fertilizers cause algae to grow too much and block sunlight. Finally, bleaching happens when the salt content gets too low, killing coral.

tilizers. The main ingredient in these fertilizers is nitrogen. When nitrogen enters the water, it has the same effect on water-dwelling vegetation (such as algae) that it has on crops: stimulating growth. That may not sound harmful, but it poses a threat to coral reefs. Excessive amounts of algae can shade coral colonies and block the sunlight. Also, as the algae growth expands, it attracts more sea creatures. They move into the area and crowd out the coral polyps as they compete for food and space.

## Protecting a Natural Work of Art

The Great Barrier Reef is a precious natural wonder created entirely by nature. But because of threats from both natural and human causes, it has suffered from serious damage. In some cases, the coral can recover and resume its growth. In others, however, it could be destroyed and lost forever. To help prevent further destruction, scientists are constantly researching the problems to determine what causes them. Their goal, in the end, is to protect the reef system and ensure its survival.

# Danger Lurks in the Reef

The Great Barrier Reef is a beautiful, captivating place. But to ship captains throughout history, it has also proven to be treacherous. It is out in the open sea, and even though some of the reefs are clearly visible, many others are hidden beneath the surface of the water. They are towering mountains of rocklike coral that rise up from the deep—and they can easily rip the entire bottoms out of ships.

## A Life-Threatening Discovery

The first European to discover the Great Barrier Reef was also involved in its first known shipwreck. In 1768 Captain James Cook sailed from his native England on a ship called *Endeavor*. Within two years he had located Australia. But he traveled more than a thousand miles up the eastern coast before he knew a reef was there—much less an immense chain of reefs.

In mid-April 1770 Cook began to see the reefs that were closest to land, but he still did not suspect that many others were far offshore. In early June the *Endeavor* crashed into one of the reefs, which tore through the ship's bottom. David Doubilet describes what happened next: "The sounds of breaking timbers, groaning and splintering, reverberated through the ship. She struck

Captain James Cook discovered the Great Barrier Reef in 1770 when his ship Endeavor crashed into one of the reefs.

[the reef] and struck fast. The waters around the Great Barrier Reef poured into her. It was sheer terror. The word 'reef' could mean a drowning death, or, worse, slow starvation about as far as humans could be—beyond the far side of the world. It was a fight for survival."[3]

Cook spotted land, and as the crew frantically bailed out water, he managed to get the crippled *Endeavor* to shore. Carpenters repaired the ship, and after several weeks of waiting for fair weather, Cook and his crew sailed again. Yet they were not out of danger. The ship was still trapped in the vast expanse of reefs, and it was totally dependent on the wind to get out. Many weeks went by before the ship was free of its coral prison. Finally, Cook saw a narrow passage through the reef. He steered the *Endeavor* through it and into the open ocean. Miraculously, no one was killed or injured during the long and dangerous ordeal.

## Chasing the *Bounty*

Twenty years later another shipwreck in the Great Barrier Reef did not have such a happy ending. A British warship called *Pandora* was sent to find the *Bounty*, a ship that had been hijacked. *Pandora*'s captain was Edward Edwards, and his mission was to bring the twenty-five hijackers (called mutineers) back to England. By March 1791 he had found and captured fourteen of the mutineers in Tahiti. They were imprisoned on the ship's deck in a cramped wooden cell that was nicknamed "Pandora's Box." Nine of the thieves were still missing, including their leader, Fletcher Christian. He had been second in command on the *Bounty* and was now at the helm of the stolen ship.

For the next four months Edwards continued to search for the *Bounty* and the rest of the mutineers, but there was no sign of them. Then disaster struck. *Pandora* was heading home to England and it ended up in a part of the Great Barrier Reef known as Torres Strait. On a stormy night in late August 1791, as Edwards tried to find the passageway out, he crashed the ship into the reef. *Pandora* quickly sank, killing four prisoners and thirty-one crew members. Many months later Edwards

The Pandora, with its cargo of mutineers, crashed into the Great Barrier Reef in 1791, killing several people on board.

and the other survivors made it back to England. The captain was found blameless in the loss of the *Pandora*, and the thieves were put on trial. Four were cleared and six were sentenced to death, although only three were actually hanged.

As for the fate of Christian and the other mutineers, they were able to escape to Pitcairn Island in the South Pacific. Once they arrived, they burned the *Bounty* to the ground so their whereabouts would not be discovered by passing vessels. The men were never found, but it is believed that they established a permanent settlement on Pitcairn Island.

## Lost in the Storm

One of the Great Barrier Reef's most tragic stories occurred in 1911. On March 23 a steel passenger and freight steamer called the *Yongala* was on its ninety-ninth voyage, captained by William Knight. With its first-class sleeping cabins, drawing room, lobby, two decks, and luxurious saloon, the *Yongala* was considered a fine ship. On this voyage it was bound for the Australian town of Cairns. Forty-nine passengers and seventy-five crew members were aboard, as well as a prize bull and a racehorse named Moonshine.

The ship was not far from land when a severe hurricane was sighted nearby. At that time, few ships had wireless communication devices on board. Although one had been ordered from England for the *Yongala*, it had not yet been installed, so Knight did not find out about the storm until it was too late. Five hours after the hurricane was reported, a lighthouse keeper watched the *Yongala* pass by, heading straight toward the storm. It was the last time the ship was ever seen.

On March 26, 1911, when the ship had not arrived at its destination, it was officially reported as missing. The Queensland government launched a massive search effort, which included seven search vessels. However, they found no trace of the ship. Then during the following weeks, wreckage from the *Yongala* began to wash up on beaches. Only one body was discovered: that of Moonshine, the

One hundred and twenty-four people died when the Yongala, a passenger and freight steamer, crashed into the Great Barrier Reef during a hurricane in 1911.

Throughout history, the many treacherous reefs of the Great Barrier Reef have caused as many as two thousand sea vessels to sink or be stranded.

horse. From that point on it was assumed that all 124 people on board had drowned.

There were many different theories about what happened to the *Yongala*. An official statement by an investigating board called it one of the "mysteries of the sea." It was assumed that the strong winds of the hurricane had capsized the ship, causing it to crash into the Great Barrier Reef. In 1947 the *Yongala*'s wreckage was discovered in eighty feet of water, but it was eleven years before divers explored the ship. To this day, no one knows for certain what caused it to sink.

## Mystery and Tragedy

The *Endeavor*, the *Pandora*, and the *Yongala* were just three of many ships that crashed in the Great Barrier Reef. Throughout history, its many treacherous reefs have claimed as many as two thousand vessels. Because of today's sophisticated navigation and communications equipment, there is very little risk of ships capsizing there. But even so, those that were lost will never be forgotten. Their spirits are as much a part of this underwater world as the thousands of living creatures that make it their home.

# Notes

**Chapter One: Miles and Miles of Coral**
1. David Doubilet, Great Barrier Reef. Washington, DC: National Geographic Insight, 2002, p. 71.
2. Quoted in Frank Talbot, ed., Reader's Digest Book of the Great Barrier Reef. Sydney, Australia: Reader's Digest, 1984, p. 9.

**Chapter Four: Danger Lurks in the Reef**
4. Doubilet, Great Barrier Reef, p. 9.

# Glossary

**atoll:** A saucer-shaped reef surrounding a lagoon and often grows on the tops of volcanoes submerged beneath the ocean.

**barrier reef:** A coral reef that runs parallel to a shoreline and is separated from land by a lagoon.

**calcium carbonate:** A limestone material found in teeth, shells, and bones.

**carbon dioxide:** A gas that occurs naturally in the atmosphere and is used in the process of photosynthesis.

**coral cay:** A low, sandy island that is formed from the compacted debris of coral and shells.

**coral polyp:** A tiny creature that is the living part of a coral reef.

**dugong:** A large marine mammal that spends its entire life in the water.

**fringing reef:** A coral reef that sometimes grows outward from the shoreline, but most often is found around islands.

**global warming:** A steady increase in the earth's average temperature.

**mollusk:** A soft-bodied marine animal, usually with a protective shell.

**nudibranch:** A shell-less member of the mollusk family.

**patch reef:** Small coral formations scattered in shallow waters.

**photosynthesis:** The food-making process of green plants.

**platform reef:** A deep-water reef that is usually circular or crescent shaped.

**ribbon reef:** Reefs that run along a shoreline and are often closer to land than other types of reefs.

**salinity:** Salt content.

**sclerites:** Tiny crystal-like structures that are found inside soft corals.

**sea anemone:** A flowerlike sea creature with stinging tentacles.

**soft coral:** A type of coral that does not have a hard skeleton (not a reef builder).

**stony coral:** The reef-building type of coral (also known as hard coral).

**zooplankton:** A microscopic sea creature that floats in the water.

**zooxanthellae:** Tiny algae that live inside stony coral polyps.

# For Further Exploration

## Books

Caroline Arnold, *A Walk on the Great Barrier Reef.* Minneapolis, MN: Carolrhoda Books, 1988. An informative book that describes the fascinating plants and animals living in the Great Barrier Reef.

Rebecca L. Johnson, *The Great Barrier Reef: A Living Laboratory.* Minneapolis, MN: Lerner, 1991. Discusses coral, the crown-of-thorns starfish, dugongs, and many other creatures that live in the reef.

## Web Sites

**Cooperative Research Centre for the Great Barrier Reef** (www.reef.crc.org.au). An excellent resource for finding information about the reef, including the different types of creatures and plants that live there.

**International Coral Reef Information Network** (www.coralreef.org). Explains the different types of coral reefs, how reefs are built, and what types of threats they face.

**Reef Futures** (www.reeffutures.org). A site that provides current information about threats to the Great Barrier Reef.

# Index

# Picture Credits

Cover Image: © Bob Charleton/Lonely Planet Images
© Bridgeman Art Library, 32, 35
Corel Corporation, 10, 13, 14, 16, 20
© Steve Drogin/SeaPics.com, 25
© Roger Hasselberg/Maritime Museum of Townsville, 37
Chris Jouan, 7, 30
© A & C Mahaney/SeaPics.com, 23
© NASA, 26
Photos.com, 19, 29
© Richard Seaman, 8
© Paul A. Souders/CORBIS, 38

# About the Author

Peggy J. Parks holds a bachelor of science degree from Aquinas College in Grand Rapids, Michigan, where she graduated magna cum laude. She is a freelance author who has written more than twenty-five books for Gale Group's KidHaven Press, Blackbirch Press, and Lucent Books. Parks lives in Muskegon, Michigan, a town she says inspires her writing because of its location on the shores of Lake Michigan.